2ND EDITION
WORKBOOK

Contents

1 Good Morning, Class! 2
2 My Family 12
3 My Body 22

Checkpoint | Units 1–3 32

4 My Favorite Clothes 34
5 Busy at Home 44
6 On the Farm 54

Checkpoint | Units 4–6 64

7 Party Time 66
8 Fun and Games 76
9 Play Time 86

Checkpoint | Units 7–9 96

Extra Grammar Practice 98
The Alphabet 107
Numbers 108

1 Good Morning, Class!

1 **Match, color, and say.**

1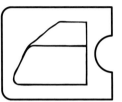

2

3

4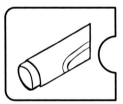

a    book

b 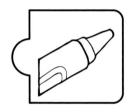   crayon

c 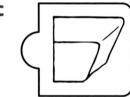   eraser

d    ruler

2 **Look and circle.**

1 What is it?

It's a **pen** / **marker**.

2 What is it?

It's a **backpack** / **desk**.

How did I do? ☆ ☆ ☆

16

3 Listen and sing. Then draw.

a

b

The Classroom Song

♪ Good morning, class.
Good morning to you!
How are you?
I'm fine, thank you.

What is it? It's an **eraser**. *(a)*
What is it? It's a **ruler**. *(b)*
What is it? It's a **pencil**. *(c)*
What is it? It's a **crayon**. *(d)*

Now pick up your pen
And open your book.
Say the words and write with me.
Let's start now. 1, 2, 3!

Chorus

c

d

4 Draw your backpack. Then color and write.

This is my _____.
It's _____.

How did I do? ☆ ☆ ☆

5 **Read and circle.**

Classroom Colors

"What is it?"

"It's **a pen / an eraser**."

"What are they?"

"They're **pencils / markers**."

6 **Listen and color.**

1

2

3

4

THINK BIG

Complete the sequence.

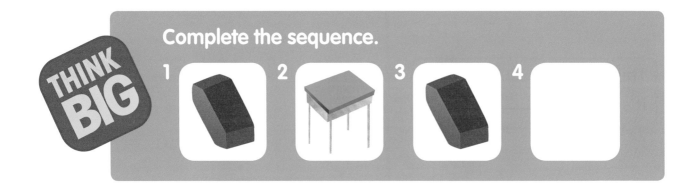

1 2 3 4

How did I do? ☆ ☆ ☆

7 ²¹ **Listen and ✓.**

1   a  ▢

     b  ▢

2   a  ▢

     b  ▢

3   a  ▢

     b  ▢

4   a  ▢

     b  ▢

8   **Read, draw, and color.**

1   It's a pencil.
    It's green.

2   It's a book.
    It's blue.

3   It's a crayon.
    It's yellow.

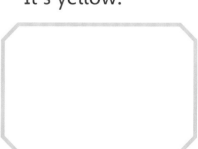

Grammar

What is it?	**It's** a ruler.
What are they?	**They're** crayons.

9 **Trace.**

What is it?

1

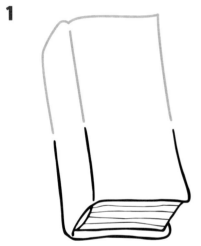

_It's_ a book.

2

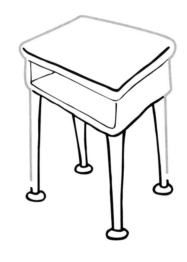

_It's_ a desk.

3

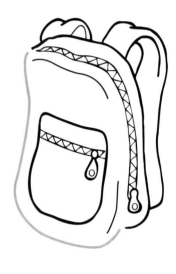

_It's_ a backpack.

10 **Listen and circle. Then color.**

1

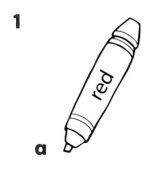

red

a

green

b

2

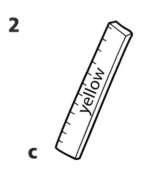

yellow

c

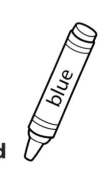

blue

d

How did I do? ☆ ☆ ☆

What are they?

They're...

11 **Match and say.**

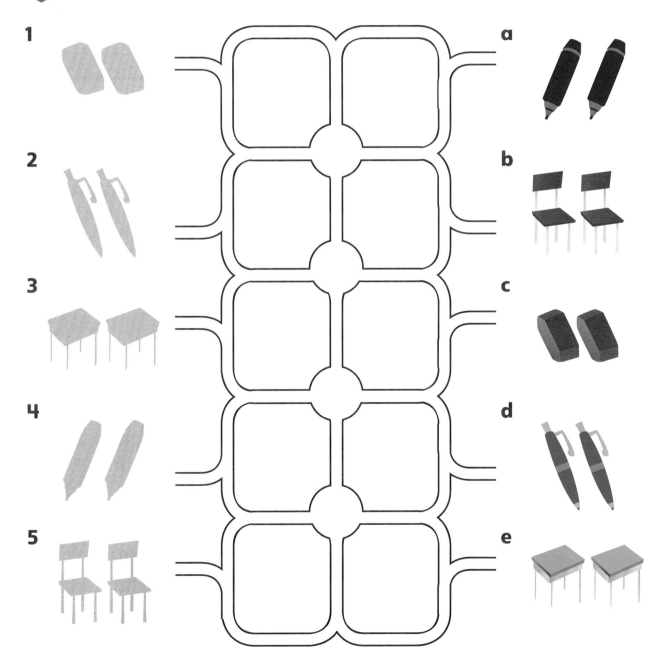

12 **Connect numbers 1 to 10. Count and write.**

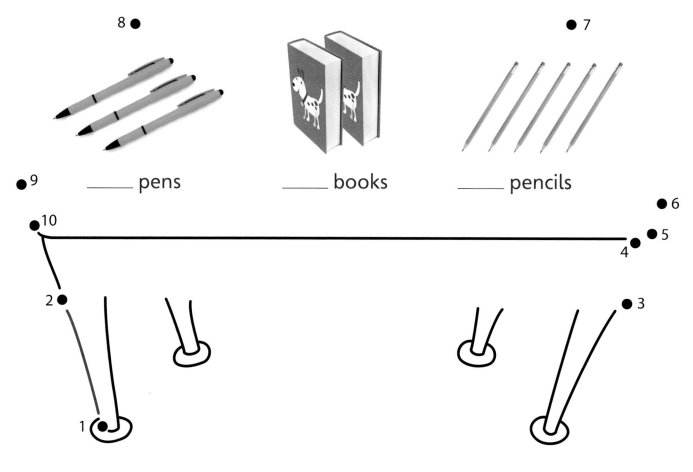

_____ pens   _____ books   _____ pencils

13 **Count and write.**

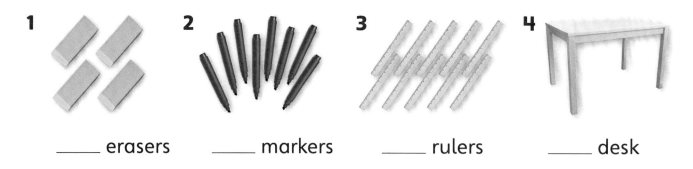

1 _____ erasers   **2** _____ markers   **3** _____ rulers   **4** _____ desk

THINK BIG

I have 3 green pens and 1 red pen.
How many pens do I have?
I have _____ pens.

How did I do? ☆ ☆ ☆

14 **Find and circle a, t, p, and n.**

a   p   c   t

o   a   p   n

s   t   n   a

15 **Read and circle a, t, p, and n.**

1 and   **2** ten   **3** pen   **4** nip

16 **Match the words with the same sounds.**

1 nap   **a** pen

2 pan   **b** and

3 ant   **c** nip

17 **Listen and chant.**
33

Pat the ant
Has a tan.
Pat the ant
Takes a nap.

18 **Read and write.**

Please   you   welcome

1

Thank you.

You're _____.

2

_____ sit down.

Thank _____.

19 **Draw.**

I'm polite in school.

How did I do? ☆☆☆

20 Read, draw, and color.

1 I have a pencil. It's yellow.

2 I have a desk. It's blue.

3 I have three markers.
  They're red.

4 I have two books.
  They're green.

21 Read and circle.

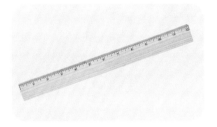

1 What is it?
  It's / They're a ruler.

2 What are they?
  It's / They're backpacks.

3 What **is it / are they**?
  It's a chair.

4 What **is it / are they**?
  They're erasers.

My Family

1 **Read and match.**

grandmother   sister   grandfather

My family.

father   brother   mother

How did I do?

43

2 Listen and circle. Then sing.

I Love My Family

My family, my family!
I love my family.
See them in this picture.
They mean so much to me.

My **father / brother**, my **mother / sister**!
My **sister / father**, my **brother / mother**!
We have so much fun.
They're number one.

My family, my family!
I love my family.
I love them and they love me,
That's why we're family!

3 Draw your mother and father. Then write.

She's my _____.   He's my _____.

How did I do? ☆ ☆ ☆

4 Read and point. Then read and circle.

A Big Family

Who are they?

That's my father and mother.

Who's she?

She's my sister.

Oh, she's Jane.

And who's he?

He's my brother!

How many brothers and sisters do I have?

I have...

a one brother and two sisters.

b one brother and one sister.

c two brothers and one sister.

THINK BIG

Look at 4 and ✓ Tim's family.

1 ☐   2 ☐

How did I do? ☆☆☆

5 Listen and write the number.

| How many brothers and sisters do you have? | I have one brother. |
| | I have two sisters. |

6 **Read, count, and color.**

How many brothers and sisters do you have?

I have two brothers.

I have one brother and two sisters.

I have three sisters.

How did I do? ☆☆☆

7 Trace and match.

How many _____ brothers and sisters do you have?

I have _____ four brothers.

I have _____ two sisters.

8 Look, read, and match.

1 **2** **3** **4**

a boy **b** man **c** woman **d** girl

51

9 Look. Then listen, read, and circle.

This is my family.

I am a ¹**boy** / **girl**. My name's Ian.

This ²**man** / **boy** is my father. This ³**girl** / **woman** is my mother.

This ⁴**boy** / **baby** is my brother. This ⁵**girl** / **boy** is my sister.

This ⁶**girl** / **woman** is my grandmother, and this is my grandfather.

THINK BIG

Are you a boy or a girl?

I'm a _____.

How did I do? ☆ ☆ ☆

10 **Find and circle i, s, b, and d.**

i   p   b   t

s   b   d   n

s   d   i   a

11 **Read and circle i, s, b, and d.**

1 dad   **2** in   **3** bat   **4** sit

12 **Match the words with the same sounds.**

1 dad   **a** sad

2 in   **b** dip

3 sit   **c** it

13 **Listen and chant.**
57

Don't sit, sit, sit
On a pin, pin, pin.
It's bad, bad, bad
To sit on a pin!

How did I do? ☆☆☆

Listen, read, and match.

1

a Tommy helps his mother. **b** Pam helps her brother.

2

15 **Draw.**

Review

16 Read and match.

She's   my brothers.

He's   my mother.

They're   my sisters.

                         my father.

17 Look, match, and say.

1

a man

2

b girl

3

c woman

4

d boy

18 Draw your family. Then say.

This is my family.

3 My Body

1 **Look and match.**

eye   head

nose   hair

foot      ear

leg   mouth

hand   fingers

toes   arm

2 **Draw your friend. Then label the parts of the body.**

How did I do? ☆ ☆ ☆

(3) **Listen and circle. Then sing.**

My Body Song

Do you have two **eyes** / **ears**?
Do you have one **mouth** / **nose**?
Do you have two eyes?
Yes, I do. Yes, I do.

I have ten **fingers** / **toes**.
I have ten toes.
I have two **hands** / **feet**
And one big nose!

And do you have long **hair** / **legs**?
And do you have short **hair** / **arms**?
And do you have small hands?
I sing my body song, my body song,
I sing my body song again!

(4) **Read and write.**

| one | ten | ten | two | two |

1 I have _____ fingers.

2 I have _____ nose.

3 I have _____ toes.

4 I have _____ ears.

5 I have _____ eyes.

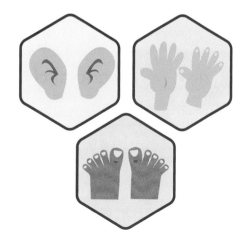

5 **Read and match.**

a Yes, he does! Bobo has one eye!

b No. My teddy bear has small ears.

Brown? Oh! Does he have one eye?

Lost Teddy Bear

Is this your teddy bear?

_____

_____

6 **Read and circle Yes or No.**

1	Is Bobo green?		Yes	No
2	Does Bobo have small ears?		Yes	No
3	Does he have long legs?		Yes	No
4	Does he have one eye?		Yes	No

THINK BIG

Read, write, and circle. Then draw.

This is _____. He's my favorite teddy bear.
He has **big / small** eyes.
He has **big / small** ears.
He has **short / long** legs.

How did I do?

7 **Read and match.**

1

It has big eyes.

2

It has short legs.

3

It has a small head.

4

It has a long neck.

8 **Listen and ✓.**

1 a

b

2 a

b

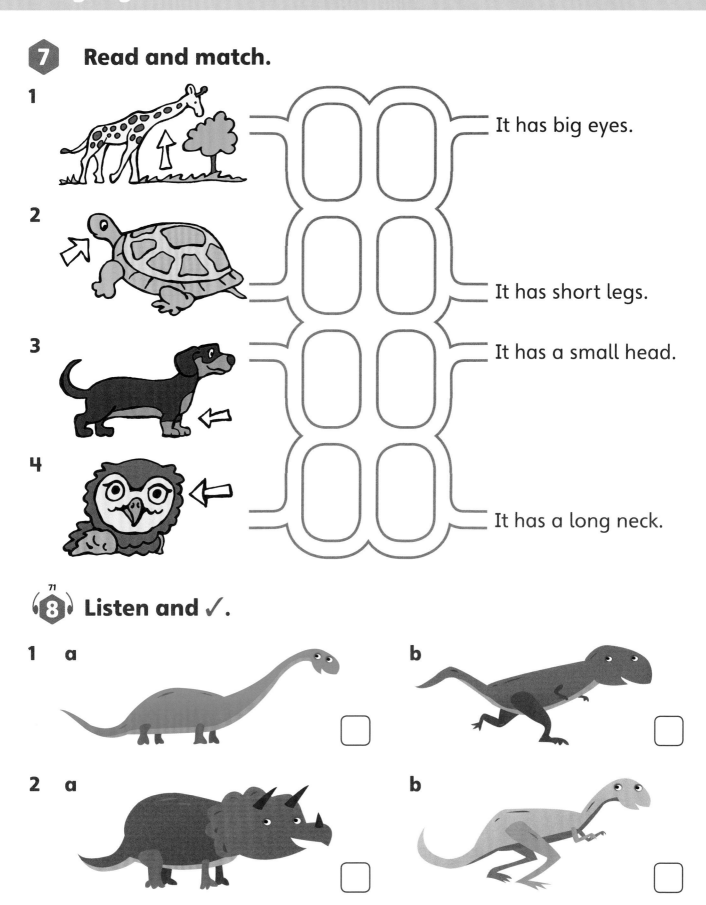

Does she **have** long hair?	Yes, she **does**.
Does he **have** short hair?	No, he **doesn't**.
Does it **have** a small head?	Yes, it **does**.
Does it **have** a big head?	No, it **doesn't**.

9 **Connect numbers 1 to 10. What is it?**

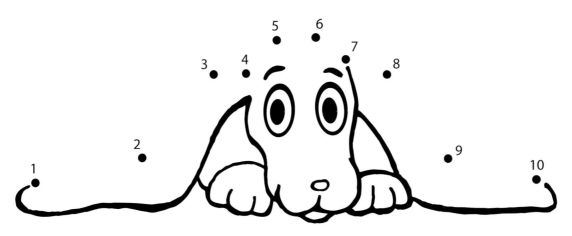

10 **Look at 9. Read and circle.**

1

Does it have long ears?

Yes, it does. / No, it doesn't.

2

Does it have small eyes?

Yes, it does. / No, it doesn't.

3

Does it have a big nose?

Yes, it does. / No, it doesn't.

How did I do? ☆☆☆

11 Read and trace.

1 Does he have
a long nose?

Yes, he does.

2 Does he have
small feet?

No, he doesn't.

3 Does he have
short hair?

Yes, he does.

12 Look at 11. Read and circle.

1 Does Meg have short hair?

Yes, she does. / No, she doesn't.

2 Does Meg have big eyes?

Yes, she does. / No, she doesn't.

How did I do? ☆☆☆

13 **Look and circle.**

1  **2**  **3**  **4**

see / hear   taste / smell   see / taste   hear / smell

75
14 **Listen, read, and write.**

a **b** 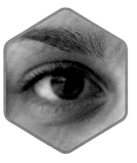 **c** 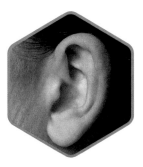 **d**

1 I hear with my ears. I hear a song.
2 I see with my eyes. I see a star.
3 I taste with my mouth. I taste ice cream.
4 I smell with my nose. I smell flowers.

THINK BIG

I see...   I smell...   I taste...   I hear...

   How did I do? ☆☆☆

15 **Find and circle e, c, g, and m.**

g   e   b   m

a   c   g   s

m   t   e   c

16 **Read and circle e, c, g, and m.**

1 gas   **2** map   **3** cap   **4** pen

17 **Match the words with the same sounds.**

1 get   **a** cat

2 mat   **b** map

3 cap   **c** gas

18 **Listen and chant.**

82

The cap is on the cat.

The cat goes on the map.

The pen goes on the bed.

How did I do? ☆ ☆ ☆

Listen and match. Then sing.

Keep Clean

1
Every day
Before I eat
And after I play,
I wash my hands.

a

2
With a lot of soap
It's easy, you see.
Rinse with water
Just like me.

b

3
Dry them well and
Sing this song.
Keep your hands clean
All day long!

c

20 **Draw.**

> I keep clean.

How did I do? ☆☆☆

21 **Read and circle.**

1 Does he have a long nose?

Yes, he does. / No, he doesn't.

2 Does he have big feet?

Yes, he does. / No, he doesn't.

3 Does he have long hair?

Yes, he does. / No, he doesn't.

22 **Look and write.** | eye   finger   leg   mouth   nose

1 _____

2 _____

3 _____

4 _____

5 _____

How did I do? ☆ ☆ ☆

1 **Look, find, and number.**

 **CLASS**

1 crayons
2 erasers
3 pens
4 rulers

2 **Look and ✓.**
Tom has:

My List

☐ pens
☐ pencils
☐ erasers
☐ a ruler

3 **Think and draw. Tom doesn't have:**

SCHOOL SUPPLIES →

BIG SALE!

4 **Work in groups and share.**

FAMILY

5	father
6	mother
7	sister

BODY

8	arm
9	eye
10	hand

My Favorite Clothes

1 **Color. Then match.**

a red blouse   blue pants   a yellow jacket

yellow boots   a blue skirt   red shoes   green gloves

2 **Draw and label.**

My Favorite Clothes

How did I do?

97
3 **Listen and circle. Then sing.**

What Are You Wearing?

What are you wearing?
I'm wearing a **T-shirt** / **shirt**.
What are you wearing?
I'm wearing a **skirt** / **blouse**.

What's he wearing?
He's wearing new **pants** / **shorts**.
What's he wearing?
He's wearing old **shoes** / **boots**.

What's she wearing?
She's wearing a **red** / **blue** hat.
What's she wearing?
She's wearing **black** / **pink** shoes.

How did I do?

4 **Match. Then read and color.**

My Favorite Hat!

1

I'm wearing a green hat. It's my favorite hat!

2

What's Tim wearing?

He's wearing a brown hat. It's his favorite hat.

3

What's Maria wearing?

She's wearing a purple hat. It's her favorite hat.

a

b

c

THINK BIG

Which clothes are the same? Circle.

How did I do? ☆ ☆ ☆

5 Listen and ✓.

1 a  **b**

2 a  **b**

3 a  **b**

4 a  **b**

6 Look, read, and circle.

I'm wearing **boots / shoes**, a hat, and a **green / yellow** jacket.

I'm wearing a **green / yellow** T-shirt, pants, and blue **boots / shoes**.

1

2

Grammar

| What **are** you **wearing**? | **I'm wearing** a green hat. |
| What's he/she **wearing**? | **He's/She's wearing** blue pants. |

7 **Color and write.**

g = **green**   b = **brown**   r = **red**   y = yellow   p = **purple**   o = orange

1 He's wearing an orange _____.

2 He's wearing a yellow _____.

3 He's wearing purple _____.

4 He's wearing brown _____.

5 He's wearing green _____.

gloves

hat

pants

shirt

shoes

38   Unit 4

How did I do?

8 **Match. Then say. Use He's wearing or She's wearing.**

1
2
3
4

a
b
c
d

9 **What are you wearing? Write.**

| orange | black | green | yellow | white | brown |

| pants | a skirt | boots | shoes | a shirt | a blouse |

1 I'm wearing _____.

2 I'm wearing _____.

3 I'm wearing _____.

10 **Look and circle.**

1
cold / hot

2
hot / dry

3
dry / wet

4
wet / cold

105
11 **Find and write. Then listen and circle.**

desert   jungle   mountains

It's cold in the
_____.
I'm wearing my
hat / T-shirt.

It's hot in the
_____.
I'm wearing my
shorts / jacket.

It's wet in the
_____.
I'm wearing my
shoes / boots.

THINK BIG

It's wet. What's she wearing? Circle.

dress   pants
        jacket   shoes
boots   shirt
        hat   gloves

How did I do? ☆ ☆ ☆

12 **Find and circle o, k, and ck.**

a   ck   c   k

th   a   sh   o

k   c   p   ck

13 **Read and circle o, k, and ck.**

1 on   **2** kid   **3** sock   **4** dog

14 **Match the words with the same sounds.**

1 pot   **a** pick

2 neck   **b** kite

3 kid   **c** dog

15 **Listen and chant.** [111]

Put on your socks,
Put on your shorts.
Kick the ball,
Kick, kick, kick!

How did I do? ☆ ☆ ☆

16 **Look, read, and write.**

dress   shirt

They're wearing traditional clothes from the Philippines. He's wearing a _____ and she's wearing a _____.

17 **Draw.**

I'm wearing traditional clothes.

How did I do? ☆ ☆ ☆

18 **Look and write.**

| blouse | boots | dress | gloves | hat |
| jacket | pants | shirt | shoes | skirt | socks |

1 _____

2 _____

3 _____

4 _____

5 _____

6 _____

7 _____

8 _____

9 _____

10 _____

11 _____

How did I do? ☆ ☆ ☆

5 Busy at Home

Vocabulary

1 **Look, read, and match.**

1 She's combing her hair. ☐

2 She's drinking, and he's reading. ☐

3 He's taking a bath. ☐

4 He's making lunch. ☐

5 He's eating. ☐

How did I do? ☆☆☆

2 **Listen and write. Then sing.**

breakfast	face	hair
lunch	phone	teeth

What Are You Doing?

I'm brushing my ¹_____.
I'm combing my ²_____.
   I'm busy. I'm busy.
   What are you doing?

I'm eating my ³_____.
I'm washing my ⁴_____.
   I'm busy. I'm busy.
   What are you doing?

I'm talking on the ⁵_____.
I'm making my ⁶_____.
   I'm busy. I'm busy.
   What are you doing?

Chorus

3 **Draw.**

He's taking a bath.	She's playing.

⬡4 Read and write.

Fun at Home

1 What are they doing?
   They're _____.

2 What is Patrick doing?
   He's _____.

3 What's she doing?
   She's _____.

THINK BIG Read, write, and draw.

We're _____
_____.

How did I do? ☆ ☆ ☆

5 **Look and color around the rooms.**

 kitchen    living room    bedroom

 bathroom    dining room

a    b

c    d    e

6 **Look at 5. Read and circle.**

1   She's in the **bathroom / bedroom**.

2   She's in the **living room / kitchen**.

3   She's in the **bedroom / dining room**.

Where's Dylan?	He**'s** in the dining room.
Where's Pam?	She**'s** in the living room.
Where are you?	I**'m** in the bedroom.

124

7 **Listen and match.**

1

2

3

4

8 **Look at 7. Write He's, I'm, or She's.**

1 Where's your father? _____ in the kitchen.

2 Where's your mother? _____ in the bedroom.

3 Where are you? _____ in the living room.

How did I do? ☆ ☆ ☆

9 **Listen. Write the number.**

10 **Look at 9. Write.**

dining room   kitchen

1 Where's Ana?

She's in the _____.

2 Where's her father?

He's in the _____.

11 **Draw. Where are you?**

I'm in the _____.

12 **Draw lines and connect the numbers. Then write.**

triangle   square   rectangle

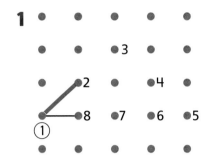

1

. . . . .
. . •3 . .
. •2 . •4 .
. •——•8 •7 •6 •5
①

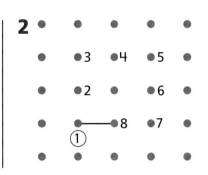

2

. . . . .
. •3 •4 •5 .
. •2 . •6 .
. •——•8 •7 .
①

3

. . . . .
•2 •3 •4 •5 •6
•——•10 •9 •8 •7
①

_____   _____   _____

13 **Count and write the number.**

1

How many circles? _____

2

How many triangles? _____

Find and draw four things in your house that are a square, a circle, a triangle, and a rectangle.

How did I do? ☆ ☆ ☆

14 **Find and circle u, f, and ff.**

ck   f   p   f

u   ff   k   s

t   ff   u   i

15 **Read and circle u, f, and ff.**

1 up   **2** fan   **3** puff   **4** bus

16 **Match the words with the same sounds.**

1 sun   **a** fan

2 off   **b** up

3 fog   **c** puff

133
17 **Listen and chant.**

We're having fun,
Running in the sun.
Up, up, up!
Puff, puff, puff!

How did I do? ☆☆☆

Listen and write.

| cleaning | drying | helping | washing |

1 She's _____ her room.

2 She's _____ the dishes.

3 He's _____ the dishes.

4 She's _____ her mom.

 Draw.

I'm helping at home.

How did I do? ☆ ☆ ☆

20 Look, read, and match.

a

b

1 I'm brushing my teeth.

2 I'm combing my hair.

3 I'm washing my face.

c

d

4 I'm eating.

5 I'm taking a bath.

e

f

6 I'm talking on the phone.

7 I'm drawing.

g

h

8 I'm reading.

9 I'm playing.

i

j

10 I'm making lunch.

How did I do? ☆ ☆ ☆

On the Farm

Vocabulary

| cow   duck   horse |

1

It's a _____.
It's **eating / flying**.

2

It's a _____.
It's **sleeping / running**.

3

It's a _____.
It's **running / flying**.

How did I do? ☆ ☆ ☆

142

2 Listen and match. Then sing.

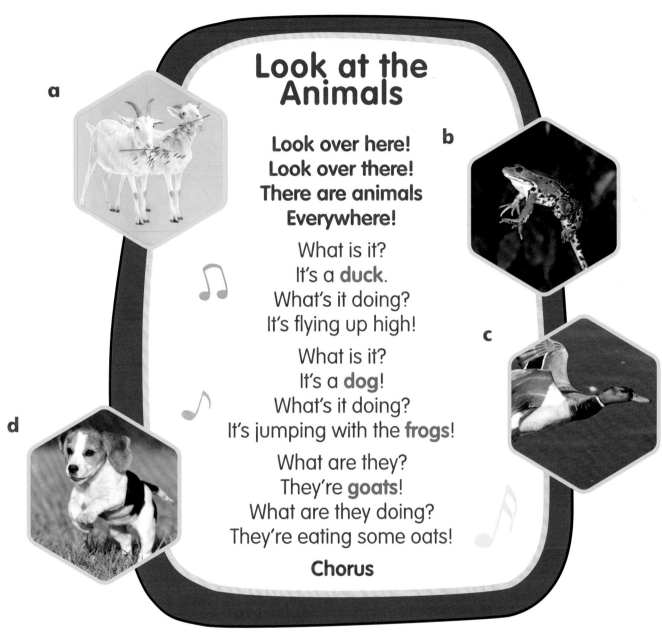

a

b

c

d

Look at the Animals

Look over here!
Look over there!
There are animals
Everywhere!

What is it?
It's a **duck**.
What's it doing?
It's flying up high!

What is it?
It's a **dog**!
What's it doing?
It's jumping with the **frogs**!

What are they?
They're **goats**!
What are they doing?
They're eating some oats!

Chorus

3 Write. Then draw.

This is my favorite
farm animal. Look.

It's a _____.

How did I do? ☆☆☆

4 Read and number.

It's Eating Your Skirt!

Oh, no! It's eating your skirt! ☐

They're running. ☐

It's jumping. ☐

It's flying. ☐

THINK BIG

Which sentence is wrong? Check (✓) or cross (✗).

The frog is jumping. ☐   The cat is flying. ☐

The horse is running. ☐

How did I do? ☆ ☆ ☆

5 **Listen and number.**

6 **Look and write.**

> eating   flying   jumping   running

1 It's _____.

2 It's _____.

3 It's _____.

4 It's _____.

How did I do? ☆ ☆ ☆

Grammar

What**'s** the duck **doing**?	It**'s swimming**.
What **are** the cows **doing**?	They**'re eating**.
What**'s** he/she **doing**?	He**'s**/She**'s running**.

7 **Look, read, and circle.**

1 It's / They're jumping.

2 It's / They're eating.

3 It's / They're flying.

4 It's / They're running.

8 **Draw.**

What's the cat doing?

It's sleeping.

How did I do? ☆ ☆ ☆

9 Look and write.

eating   flying   jumping   running   sleeping

What are they doing?

1 They're

_____.

2 It's

_____.

3 They're

_____.

4 It's

_____.

5 They're

_____.

Listen. Then color, match, and circle.

1 This cow is...   **2** This hen is...   **3** This dog is...   **4** This cat is...

a    **b**    **c**    **d**

A baby hen is called a **calf** / **chick**.

A baby dog is called a **kitten** / **puppy**.

A baby cat is called a **calf** / **kitten**.

A baby cow is called a **puppy** / **calf**.

11 **What's your favorite baby animal? Write and draw.**

My favorite baby animal is a _____.

A _____ is a baby _____.

THINK BIG

Circle the picture that is wrong.

a    **b**    **c**

How did I do? ☆ ☆ ☆

12 **Find and circle r, h, and j.**

g   h   r   j

a   h   o   t

m   r   j   c

13 **Read and circle r, h, and j.**

1 rat   **2** hat   **3** jam   **4** run

14 **Match the words with the same sounds.**

1 red   **a** hut

2 hen   **b** rock

3 jam   **c** job

15 **Listen and chant.** 156

A red hen in
A red hat
Is eating red jam.
Run, red hen, run!

16 **Listen and match. Then write.**

| brushing | feeding | playing | walking |

a

☐

b

☐

c

☐

d

☐

1 I'm _____ the dog.　　**2** I'm _____ with the cat.

3 I'm _____ the hens.　　**4** I'm _____ the horse.

17 **Draw.**

I'm playing with the cat.

How did I do? ☆ ☆ ☆

18 **Look, read, and circle.**

1

1 It's a **dog** / **cat**.

2

2 It's a **goat** / **dog**.

3

3 It's a **cow** / **sheep**.

4

4 It's a **frog** / **sheep**.

5

5 It's a **turtle** / **horse**.

6

6 It's a **chicken** / **horse**.

19 **Listen and ✓. Then write.**

161

flying	jumping	swimming

1 a

b

They're _____.

2 a

b

It's _____.

3 a

b

They're _____.

How did I do? ☆ ☆ ☆

1 **Look, find, and number.**

CLOTHES

1 dress
2 shoes
3 pants
4 shirt

2 **Look and ✓.**
What is Sue wearing?

- [ ] a hat
- [ ] a T-shirt
- [ ] boots
- [ ] pants
- [ ] a jacket

3 **Look at 1 and draw.**
What other animals can you see?

4 **Work in groups and share.**

AT HOME

5 reading
6 talking on
  the phone
7 drinking

ANIMALS

8 cat
9 duck
10 turtle

7 Party Time

Vocabulary

1 **Match.**

1

2

milk	grapes
a	**b**
c	**d**
juice	pizza

3

4

2 **Look at 1. Write.**

1 She has _____.

2 He has _____.

3 They have _____.

4 She has _____.

How did I do? ☆ ☆ ☆

168
3 Listen and number. Then sing.

a

b

It's My Birthday Party!

Welcome, friends.
Please sit down.
It's my birthday party!
With games and a clown!

We have pizza, **hot dogs**,
Salad, too.
Apples, **cake**,
And **ice cream** for you!

c

d

Or put a **hamburger**
On your plate.
With juice or **milk**
It'll taste great.

e

Thanks for the presents.
What a great day!
Let's eat and drink
And play, play, play.

f

4 Draw.

I have pizza, salad, and juice.

5 Read and write.

How Many More Days?

Today is Saturday. It's my party!

Mmm! I have pizza! What do you have?

I have chicken and salad.

1 Tim's party is on _____.

2 Tim has _____.

What does Maria have?

She has pasta.

Oh, no! He has cake and ice cream!

Patrick!

3 Maria has _____.

4 Patrick has _____ and _____.

THINK BIG

Write the days in order. What day is it today? Circle.

_____ Monday _____ _____

Thursday _____ Saturday

How did I do? ☆ ☆ ☆

6   **Look and write.**

I have apples and oranges.   I have pizza.

What do you have?

1 _____

2 _____

7   **Read and draw.**

1 I have salad and hot dogs.

2 I have ice cream and fruit.

How did I do?   ☆ ☆ ☆

Grammar

What **does** he **have**?	He **has** milk.
What **do** you **have**?	I **have** juice.

8 **Look and match. Then write.**

cake   grapes   ice cream   an apple   a hot dog

1   **2**   **3**   **4**   **5**

1 What does he have?   He has _____.

2 What does she have?   She has _____.

3 What does he have?   He _____.

4 What does he have?   _____

5 What does she have?   _____

How did I do?   ☆ ☆ ☆

9 Listen and match. Then write.

1 I have pizza.

2 I _____.

pizza · a salad · juice · a sandwich · a hamburger

3 I _____.

4 I _____.

5 I _____.

10 Look and write.

1 What does he have?

He has a _____

and _____.

2 What does she have?

She has a _____

and _____.

11 **Look and write.**

| chips | chocolate | cookies | fries | salt | sugar |

1 _____

2 _____

3 _____

4 _____

5 _____

6 _____

12 **Listen, read, and circle.**

Some foods are salty, and some are sweet.
Chocolate is my favorite ¹**salty / sweet** food, and
pizza is my favorite ²**salty / sweet** food.

Fries are ³**salty / sweet**, and chips are ⁴**salty / sweet**,
too. They have ⁵**salt / sugar** on them.

Cookies, cake, and ice cream are all ⁶**salty / sweet**.
They have ⁷**salt / sugar** in them.

THINK BIG

Draw and write.

_____ sweet.

_____ salty.

How did I do? ☆ ☆ ☆

13 **Find and circle l, ll, v, and w.**

i   l   v   o

ll   t   a   v

t   w   l   p

14 **Read and circle l, ll, v, and w.**

1 van   **2** leg   **3** web   **4** doll

15 **Match the words with the same sounds.**

1 let   **a** sell

2 bell   **b** leg

3 vet   **c** win

4 we   **d** van

16 **Listen and chant.** 181

Let's ring the bell
For the vet
With the van!

How did I do? ☆☆☆

17 **Write.**

Birthday   Father's Day   New Year

1

Happy _____!

Thank you. Happy New Year to you!

2

Happy _____!
I have a present for you.

Thank you.

3

Happy _____,
Dad!

Thank you. It's in one more day!

18 **Choose and draw.**

It's...

- my birthday.

- Father's Day.

- New Year's Day.

How did I do? ☆ ☆ ☆

19 **Look and write questions and answers.**

1 What _____ you have? I have _____.

2 What does he _____? He has _____.

3 What _____ she _____? _____ has juice.

20 **Color. Then match and read.**

1 I have   **a** apples.

2 Mom has   **b** cake.

3 Dad has    **c** ice cream.

21 **Read and circle.**

1 We **have / has** a pet.

2 Sally **have / has** soup on her birthday.

3 My grandmother **have / has** five hens.

4 My dog **have / has** four puppies.

Fun and Games

Vocabulary

 1 **Listen and number.**

a   b   c

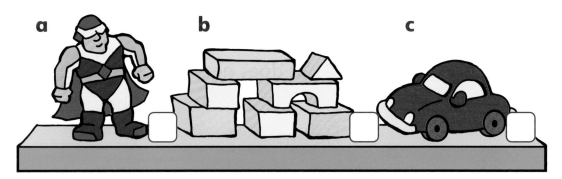

d   e   f

2 **Look at 1. Write.**

| action figure   ball   blocks   car   puppet   train |

a This is my _____.   **b** These are my _____.

c This is my _____.   **d** This is my _____.

e This is my _____.   **f** This is my _____.

         How did I do? ☆ ☆ ☆

190
3 **Listen and circle. Then sing.**

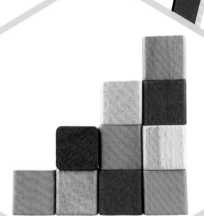

What's In Your Toy Box?

Kim, what's in your toy box?
Do you have an **airplane** / **bike**?
No, but this is my blue **car** / **game**.
And where's my gray train?

Kim, what's on your toy shelf?
Do you have a **ball** / **doll**?
Yes, yes, here it is.
And here's my purple **doll** / **car**.

Kim, what's on your table?
Do you have **big blocks** / **stuffed animals**?
Yes, and these are my **puppets** / **trains**.
My favorite's Mr. Fox!

These are my favorite toys,
Purple, green, and gray.
I share my toys with my friends.
And I play every day!

4 **Draw toys.
Then write.**

This is my

_____

and my

_____.

How did I do? ☆ ☆ ☆

5 **Read and circle.**

Where Are My Toys?

1 Where's the doll?

It's **in / under** the table.

2 Where are the action figures?

They're **on / under** the couch.

THINK BIG Look. Circle three differences.

How did I do? ☆ ☆ ☆

6 **Read and number.**

1 It's under the desk.

2 They're on the shelf.

3 It's in the toy box.

a

b

c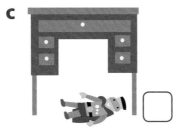

7 **Write in, on, or under.**

1 _____

2 _____

3 _____

4 _____

5 _____

6 _____

8 **Read and draw.**

The book is on the table.

The cat is under the table.

| **Where**'s the ball? | It's **in** the toy box.
It's **on** the shelf.
It's **under** the table. |
| **Where** are the skates? | They're **under** the desk.
They're **on** the couch. |

195

1 **Listen and circle in, on, or under.**

1	in	on	**2**	on	under	**3**	on	under
4	in	on	**5**	on	in	**6**	under	on

How did I do? ☆☆☆

10 **Join and draw.**

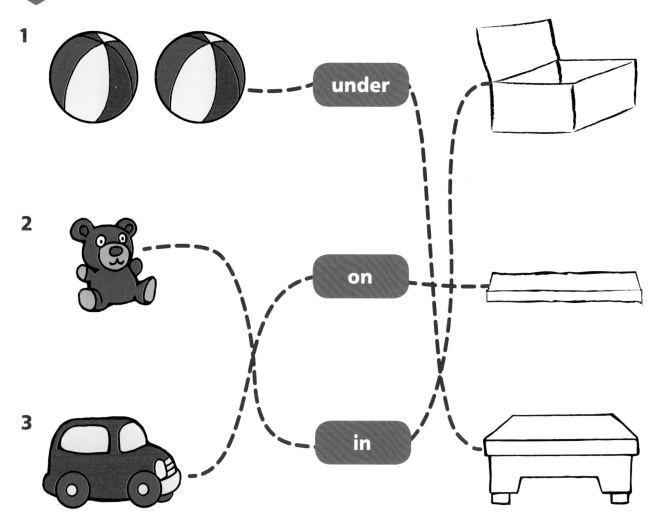

11 **Look at 10 and circle.**

1 Where are the balls?

The balls are **in / on / under** the table.

2 Where is the stuffed animal?

The stuffed animal is **in / on / under** the toy box.

3 Where is the car?

The car is **in / on / under** the shelf.

12 **Trace.**

11   12   13   14   15
16   17   18   19   20

13 **Count and write. How many?**

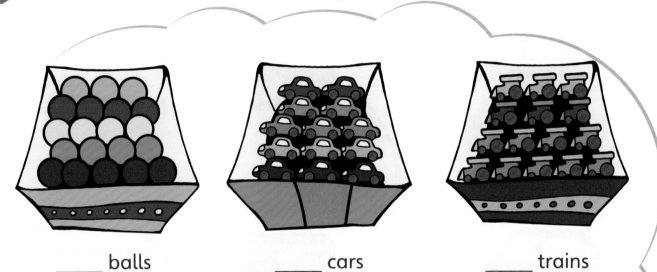

____ balls   ____ cars   ____ trains

____ airplanes   ____ games

How did I do? ☆ ☆ ☆

14 **Find and circle qu, x, and y.**

pi   p   qu   x   s

x   g   w   s   y

i   j   qu   hu   y

15 **Read and circle qu, x, and y.**

1 six   **2** quick   **3** yell   **4** box

16 **Match the words with the same sounds.**

1 quick   **a** yes

2 fox   **b** box

3 yum   **c** quack

17  **Listen and chant.**

Six quick foxes,
In a yellow box!

How did I do? ☆ ☆ ☆

18 **Match.**

a  b  c

1 OK. Thank you!

2 Sharing is fun!

3 Here's my car. Let's share.

19 **Draw.**

Here's my

_____.

Let's share.

How did I do? ☆ ☆ ☆

20 Look and match. Then read.

John's toys

1

2

3

4

5

a action figure

b ball

c blocks

d airplane

e bike

21 Listen and number.

22 Look at 21. Count and write.

How many toys can you see? I can see _____ toys.

9 Play Time

Vocabulary

1 Follow the path. Write.

catching	dancing	hitting
jumping	kicking	riding
singing	skating	throwing

1 _____

2 _____

3 _____

4 _____

5 _____

6 _____

7 _____

8 _____

9 _____

How did I do? ☆ ☆ ☆

211
2 **Listen and sing. Then match.**

1

2

3

4

Play Time Is Cool!

We like play time at our school.
Singing and dancing,
Throwing and catching.
Play time is cool at our school!

I'm throwing the ball.
It's so much fun!
Are you hitting and running?
Yes, and it's fun.

We're kicking the ball
And trying to score.
It's so much fun.
Let's play some more.

Chorus

3 **Look at 2 and write.**

1 She is _____ the ball.   **2** He is _____ the ball.

3 She is _____ .   **4** She is _____ the ball.

4 **What are you doing? Draw and write.**

I'm _____

_____ .

5 **Read and write.**

I'm Not Tired!

1

Is Patrick sleeping?

No, he isn't. He's jumping on the bed.

2

Are they sleeping now?

No, they aren't. They're dancing.

3

It's quiet now! Are they sleeping?

Yes, they are!

1 What's Patrick doing in picture 1?

He's _____.

2 What are the boys doing in picture 2?

They're _____.

3 What are the boys doing in picture 3?

They're _____.

THINK BIG

Think, write, and draw!

Look at me. I'm _____.

How did I do? ☆ ☆ ☆

6 **Look and ✓.**

Is Tom skating?

Yes, he is.
No, he isn't.

Is Jen jumping?

Yes, she is.
No, she isn't.

7 **Look and write.**

Yes, it is.   No, it isn't.

1

Is it playing?

_____

2

Is it singing?

_____

3

Is it sleeping?

_____

Grammar

| Is she singing? | Yes, she is. | No, she isn't. |
| Are they dancing? | Yes, they are. | No, they aren't. |

8 Listen and number.

9 Look at 8. Count and write.

1 How many are jumping? _____
2 How many are singing? _____
3 How many are throwing a ball? _____
4 How many are having play time? _____

How did I do? ☆ ☆ ☆

10 Look, listen, and circle.

1

Yes, he is. / No, he isn't.

2

Yes, she is. / No, she isn't.

3

Yes, they are. / No, they aren't.

4

Yes, they are. / No, they aren't.

11 Look and write.

1

Are they playing?

Yes, _____.

2

Are they kicking a ball?

No, _____.

12 **Look and match.**

1 hide and seek

2 climbing

3 tag

4 jumping rope

5 hopscotch

a

b

c

d

e

13 **Listen, read, and write.**

| climbing | hide and seek | hopscotch | jump rope | tag |

1 Katie and Simon are playing _____. I'm playing, too. It's our favorite game. Hop! Hop! Hop!

2 Emily is _____ the tree. Up! Up! She's at the top! It's very high.

3 The boys are playing _____ on the school playground. George is looking for his friends. Where are they?

4 Tom and Dan are playing _____ with my brother. Run, Dan! Run! Tag, you're it, Tom!

5 My sisters _____ on the playground. It's a lot of fun. Jump! Jump! Jump!

THINK BIG

What games do you play? Write.

|_____.

How did I do? ☆☆☆

14 **Find and circle ss, z, and zz.**

s   j   o   ss   t

p   z   qu   s   zz

ll   e   ss   x   z

15 **Read and circle ss, z, and zz.**

1 fizz   **2** mess   **3** zap   **4** miss

16 **Match the words with the same sounds.**

1 zip   **a** zap
2 buzz   **b** hiss
3 miss   **c** fizz

228
17 **Listen and chant.**

Buzz goes the bee.
Zip, zap!
It misses me!

How did I do? ☆☆☆

18 **Write. Match.**

catching   reading   eating   running   washing   swimming

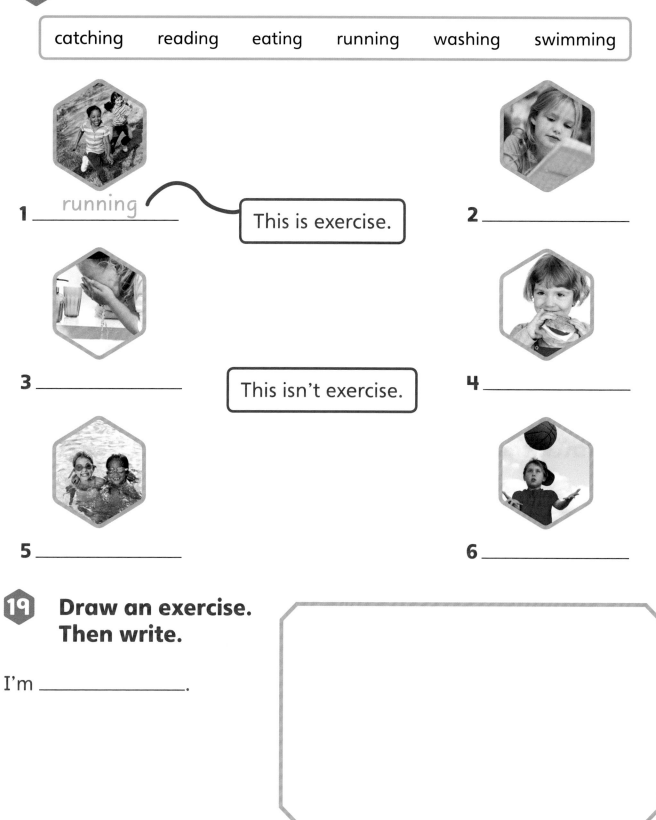

1 _running_ ___

This is exercise.

2 ___

3 ___

This isn't exercise.

4 ___

5 ___

6 ___

19 **Draw an exercise. Then write.**

I'm ___.

How did I do? ☆ ☆ ☆

20 **Listen and number. Then write.**

1 Is she jumping? No she _____. She's singing.

2 Is he hitting the ball? No, he isn't. He's _____ the ball.

3 Is she _____ the ball? Yes, she is.

4 Are they dancing? No they _____. They're skating.

5 Is he _____ rope? Yes, he is.

How did I do? ☆ ☆ ☆

1 Look, find, and number.    TOYS

1 action figure
2 bike
3 game
4 puppet

2 Look and ✓. What does he have?

My Party List

☐ cars
☐ a bike
☐ a game
☐ a puppet
☐ a train

3 Think and draw. What is in the present?

4 Work in groups and share.

🔍 PARTY FOOD

5 cake

6 fruit

7 juice

🔍 PLAY TIME

8 catching

9 kicking

10 throwing

What is it?	It**'s** a ruler.
What are they?	They**'re** crayons.

1 Write and color.

1 What is it?  _____ a marker. It's blue.

2 What _____ it?  _____ a ruler. It's yellow.

3 _____ is it?  _____ a backpack. It's red.

4 What is _____?  _____ a crayon. It's green.

5 _____ _____ it?  _____ a pencil. It's blue.

6 What _____ _____?  _____ a book. It's red.

2 Join. Then look and circle.

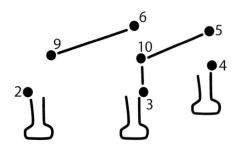

What is it?

It's a **chair** / **desk**.

How did I do? ☆☆☆

Extra Grammar Practice

How many brothers and sisters **do** you **have**?

I **have** one brother.

I **have** two sisters.

---

1 **Write and match.**

1 I _____ three sisters.

a

2 I _____ two brothers.

b

3 I _____ one brother and one sister.

c

4 I _____ one sister.

d

5 I _____ two sisters and one brother.

e

2 **Draw a monster family.**

3 **Look at 2. Count and write.**

How many monsters? _____

Extra Grammar Practice

Does she **have** long hair?	Yes, she **does**.
Does he **have** short hair?	No, he **doesn't**.
Does it **have** a small head?	Yes, it **does**.
Does it **have** a big head?	No, it **doesn't**.

1 Look and match.

1 Does she have a long nose?

2 Does she have short hair?

3 Does she have long arms?

4 Does she have big feet?

5 Does he have a long nose?

6 Does he have short hair?

7 Does he have long arms?

8 Does he have big feet?

Yes, she does.

No, she doesn't.

Yes, he does.

No, he doesn't.

2 Look and write.

1 It has a big _____.
2 It has long _____.

How did I do? ☆ ☆ ☆

Extra Grammar Practice

| What **are** you **wearing**? | **I'm wearing** a green hat. |
| What**'s** he/she **wearing**? | He**'s**/She**'s wearing** white pants. |

1 **What's she wearing? Write and color.**

1 _____ a red blouse.

2 _____ a yellow skirt.

3 _____ brown shoes.

2 **Read and color.**

What are you wearing?

I'm wearing a red jacket and brown pants.

I'm wearing an orange dress and purple shoes.

Extra Grammar Practice

Where's Dylan?	He**'s** in the dining room.
Where's Pam?	She**'s** in the living room.
Where are you?	I**'m** in the bedroom.

1 **Look and write He's or She's.**

1 Where's Jim?

_____ in the kitchen.

2 Where's Ellen?

_____ in the bedroom.

3 Where's Ben?

_____ in the bathroom.

4 Where's Pam?

_____ in the living room.

2 **Look at 1. Write.**

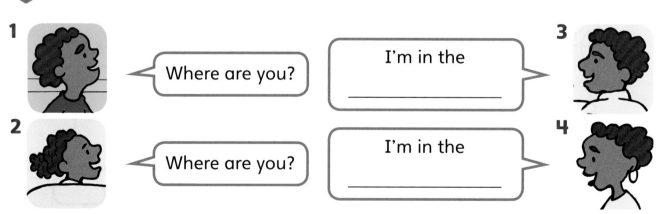

1 Where are you?

I'm in the _____

2 Where are you?

I'm in the _____

How did I do? ☆☆☆

Extra Grammar Practice

What**'s** the duck **doing**?	It**'s swimming**.
What **are** the cows **doing**?	They**'re eating**.
What**'s** he/she **doing**?	He**'s**/She**'s running**.

1 **Look and match. What are they doing?**

1

           a sleeping

2

           b running

3

           c swimming

4

           d eating

2 **Read. Circle and write.**

1 What's he doing? 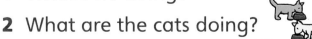 He's / They're _____.

2 What are the cats doing?  She's / They're _____.

3 What's she doing? She's / He's _____.

4 What's it doing? It's / They're _____.

Extra Grammar Practice

What **does** he **have**?	He **has** milk.
What **do** you **have**?	I **have** juice.

1 **Look, read, and circle.**

1 What does he have? He has **cake** / **milk**.

2 What does she have? She has **an apple** / **salad**.

3 What do you have? I have **pizza** / **a hot dog**.

4 What do they have? They have **grapes** / **juice**.

2 **Write has or have. Then match.**

1 I _____ juice. **a**

2 She _____ salad. **b**

3 They _____ fries. **c**

4 He _____ ice cream. **d**

How did I do? ☆ ☆ ☆

Extra Grammar Practice

Where's the ball?	It's **in** the toy box. It's **on** the shelf. It's **under** the table.
Where are the skates?	They're **under** the desk. They're **on** the couch.

1   **Write Where's or Where are. Then match.**

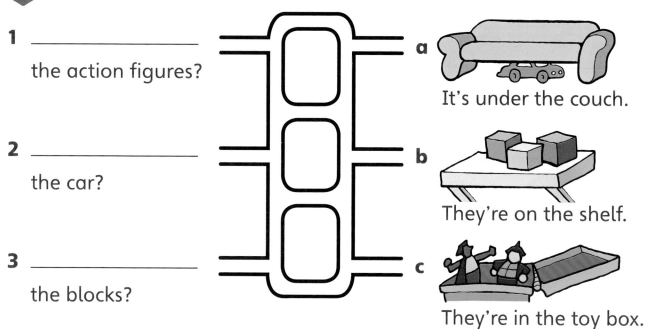

1 _____

the action figures?

2 _____

the car?

3 _____

the blocks?

a

It's under the couch.

b

They're on the shelf.

c

They're in the toy box.

2   **Look and write in, on, or under.**

1 Where's the ball?

It's _____ the desk.

2 Where are the balls?

They're _____ the desk.

3 Where's the ball?

It's _____ the desk.

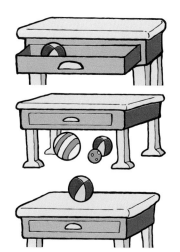

How did I do?   ☆ ☆ ☆

| **Is** she **singing**? | Yes, she **is**. | No, she **isn't**. |
| **Are** they **dancing**? | Yes, they **are**. | No, they **aren't**. |

1 **Look, read, and write.**

1
Is she throwing the ball?
Yes, she
_____.

2
Is he singing?
No, he
_____.

3
Are they sleeping?
No, they
_____.

4
Are they jumping rope?
Yes, they
_____.

2 **Look at 1. Write Is or Are. Then answer.**

1 _____ she eating?
_____

2 _____ he reading?
_____

3 _____ they climbing?
_____

4 _____ they running?
_____

How did I do? ☆ ☆ ☆

Trace.

A a   B b   C c

D d   E e   F f

G g   H h   I i

J j   K k   L l

M m   N n   O o

P p   Q q   R r

S s   T t   U u

V v   W w   X x

Y y   Z z

How did I do? ☆ ☆ ☆

Trace.

1   2   3

4   5   6

7   8   9

10   11   12

13   14   15

16   17   18

19   20

How did I do? ☆ ☆ ☆

Pearson Education Limited

KAO Two
KAO ParkHarlow
Essex
CM17 9NA
England
and Associated Companies throughout the world.

English.com/BigEnglish2

© Pearson Education Limited 2017

Authorised adaptation from the United States edition entitled Big English, 1st Edition, by Mario Herrera and Christopher Sol Cruz. Published by Pearson Education Inc. © 2013 by Pearson Education, Inc.

The right of Mario Herrera and Christopher Sol Cruz to be identified as the authors of this Work have been asserted by them in accordance with the Copyright, Designs and Patents Act 1988.

All rights reserved; no part of this publication may be reproduced, stored in a retrieval system, or transmitted in any form or by any means, electronic, mechanical, photocopying, recording, or otherwise without the prior written permission of the Publishers.

First published 2017
Sixteenth impression 2023
ISBN: 978-1-2922-3322-2

Set in Heinemann Roman

Printed in Slovakia by Neografia

Acknowledgements

Picture Credits

The publisher would like to thank the following for their kind permission to reproduce their photographs:

(Key: b-bottom; c-centre; l-left; r-right; t-top)

123RF.com: 6, 13, 86/9, 89r, BlueOrange Studio 63/2 (b), bryljaev 8tl, Andreja Donko 8tc, dotshock 40cr, Racorn 62tl; **Alamy Stock Photo:** Agencja Fotograficzna Caro 52tl, Arco Images GmbH 55tr, 57tl, Cultura Creative 66bl, Imagemore Co Ltd 40cl, Semen Lihodeev 43/2, Jurgen Magg 91l, 106bl, Anna Maloverjan 40c, Jeff Morgan 91r, 106br, OJO Images Ltd 74br, Tetra Images 52br; **BananaStock:** 53 (a); **Corbis:** Hero Images 52tr; **Fotolia.com:** byrdyak 63/6, dimedrol68 5/2 (b), fir4ik 28/2, ftfoxfoto 60tr, gena96 72/6, Gradt 71tc, heros1973 67tl, iofoto 94tl, iordani 53 (f), Michael Ireland 86/2, 106tl, jjpixs 86/3, jo 40/4, kilukilu 43/7, Konovalov Pavel 43/4, Kzenon 53 (c), Chris Leachman 72/3, Delmas Lehman 63/3 (a), Pavel Losevsky 28/1, magann 40/1, Maria Mitrofanova 43/6, Monkey Business 72tr, Natika 72/5, nbiebach 63/1, Alexandr Ozerov 40/2, picsfive 72/2, PictureArt 23, pio3 86/6, rakjung2 63/5, Atiketta Sangasaeng 5/1 (b), 8/4, Schlierner 5/2 (a), Sentello 53 (b), 94cl, simmittorok 5/1 (a), 11bl, sommersby 43/9, sumnersgraphicsinc 72tl, Rudolf Tepfenhart 40br, The Josh 40/3, Vitaly Tiagunov 43/11, Vaida 60br, vgm6 60bc, Viktor 72/4, 72cl, Ivonne Wierink 5/3 (b), 11tr, windu 43/5, xalanx 62bl, Joanna Zielinska 86/8, 89tl; **Getty Images:** Paul Bradbury 53 (i), 94tr, Digital Vision 53 (j), Digital Vision / Kraig Scarbinsky 52bl, Fuse 53 (d), sdominick 22, Urilux 63/1 (a); **Pearson Education Ltd:** Studio 8 53 (h), Trevor Clifford 7l, 7r, 26t, 26c, 26b, 74tl, 74tr, 74cl, 74cr, 74bl; **Shutterstock.com:** 67tr, 71r, 71bc, Bragin Alexey 72/1, all_about_people 53 (e), Ilya Andriyanov 28 (a), AnetaPics 55bl, Anneka 60tc (left), Ingvar Bjork 8/2, Tatiana Bobkova 62tr, Brenda Carson 67bl, DenisNata 66tl, 75r, Digital Media Pro 28/4, Dragon Images 42, Risteski Goce 94cr, Volodymyr Goinyk 40bl, Golden Pixels LLC 62br, 94bl, greenland 86/7, 106tr, Ruslan Guzov 12, 18, haveseen 53 (g), Horiyan 67br, Mau Horng 72cr, Eric Isselee 55tl, 55tc, Joseph 28 (b), Karkas 43/3, 43/8, Aleksandr S Khachuts 28 (c), Tania Kolinko 75c, Joana Kruse 66br, Lisovskaya Natalia 5/3 (a), Alexey Losevich 40b, Luchschen 71l, Alexander Mak 60tc (right), Makarova Viktoria 54c, 57bl, mathom 60tl, michaeljung 35, Monkey Business Images 28 (d), 66tr, 75l, Morgan Lane Photography 63/1 (b), Pavel V Mukhin 43/1, Amy Myers 86/4, Olga Nayashkova 71cl, Martin Nemec 54t, 57br, 60bl, 63/3, Nenov Brothers Images 77, Michal Ninger 54b, 55br, 57tr, 63/3 (b), M. Unal Ozmen 72b, PhotoNAN 43/10, Randy Rimland 63/4, Karen Roach 5/4 (a), 8/3, 11tl, 67cl, Anna Sedneva 55 (oats), Valery Shklovskiy 63/2, Margaret M Stewart 5/4 (b), 8/1, 11br, studio online 67cr, Mike Tan 63/2 (a), Christophe Testi 8tr, Leah-Anne Thompson 86/1, 94br, Matt Tilghman 40bc; **SuperStock:** 28/3; **www.imagesource.com:** 86/5

Cover images: *Front:* **Getty Images:** mrs

All other images © Pearson Education

Illustrated by

April Hartmann, Steve Mack, Zaharias Papadopoulos, Jose Rubio, Christos Skaltsas, Mike Wesley.

Every effort has been made to trace the copyright holders and we apologise in advance for any unintentional omissions. We would be pleased to insert the appropriate acknowledgement in any subsequent edition of this publication.